CROWDFUNDING FOR SOCIAL GOOD

WORKBOOK

DEVIN D. THORPE

©Copyright 2017 Devin D. Thorpe

All rights reserved. No part of this book may be reproduced or utilized, in any form or by any means, electronic or mechanical, without prior permission in writing from the publisher.

Crowdfunding for Social Good Workbook

ISBN: 1544056397

ISBN-13: 978-1544056395

Additional copies of this workbook and its companion book, *Crowdfunding for Social Good, Financing Your Mark on the World* are available from Amazon.com and BarnesAndNoble.com.

Scan the QR code to visit Devin Thorpe's author page on Amazon.com where you can see purchase any of his books, including additional copies of this workbook and its companion book, *Crowdfunding for Social Good, Financing Your Mark on the World* or just enter bit.ly/devinonamazon.

My Notes

Date:_____

_____

_____

_____

_____

_____

_____

_____

_____

_____

_____

_____

_____

_____

_____

_____

DEVIN THORPE

Crowdfunding Speaker

To check Devin's availability, call 801-930-0588 or send an email to speaker@devinthorpe.com.

Crowdfunding for Social Good

Devin Thorpe is a crowdfunding speaker who speaks primarily about crowdfunding for social good. Drawing from his book of the same title, Devin helps nonprofit audiences learn how to add crowdfunding to their annual development plans and teaches other social entrepreneurs to use crowdfunding to launch or growth their social enterprises.

- You will learn to assess your own crowdfunding prospects before you begin
- You will discover how you can reach one-third of your goal on the first day of your campaign
- You will see how you can get the media to share your crowdfunding story

Champion of Social Good

Devin Thorpe was a finance guy until he realized life wasn't all about the money. As a new-media journalist and founder of the Your Mark on the World Center, Devin has established himself as a champion of social good. As a Forbes contributor, with 400 bylines and over one million unique visitors, he has become a recognized name in the social impact arena. His YouTube show, Your Mark on the World, featuring over 700 celebrities, CEOs, billionaires, entrepreneurs and others who are out to change the world, features frequent crowdfunding guests. He is the author of *Crowdfunding for Social Good, Financing Your Mark on the World.*

Previously, Devin served as the CFO of the third largest company on the 2009 Inc. 500 list. He also founded and led an NASD-registered investment bank. After completing a degree in finance at the University of Utah, he earned an MBA from Cornell University.

Having lived on three continents and visited over 40 countries on six continents and with guests from around the world on his show, Devin brings a global perspective to audiences around the world–from the UN to Nepal–empowering them to do more good and make their mark on the world. These lessons also enable them to change their personal lives and to drive positive change within their organizations.

Take less than two minutes to watch a short video about the Endless Computer's crowdfunding success.

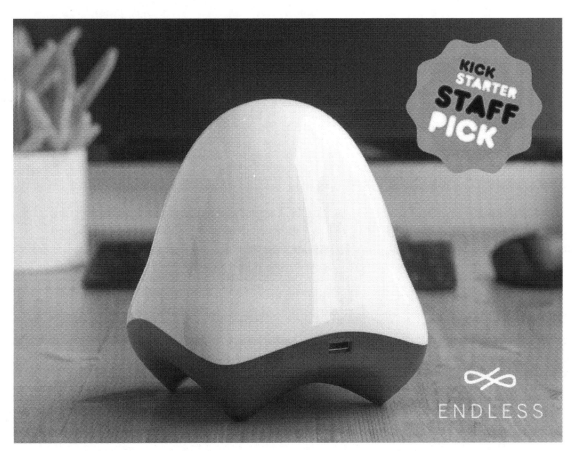

To watch the video, scan the QR code at the left or visit:

youtu.be/uV0-e79dU9A.

Definition:

Crowdfunding is the use of third-party websites to raise money from the public.

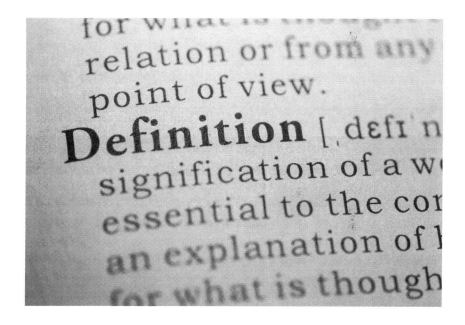

Types of Crowdfunding:

Donations

_____

_____

_____

Rewards

_____

_____

_____

Investments

_____

_____

_____

Take less than two minutes to watch a short video about Sam's Birthmark's crowdfunding success.

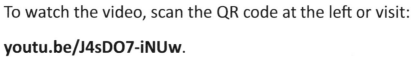

To watch the video, scan the QR code at the left or visit:

youtu.be/J4sDO7-iNUw.

Timeline—Reconnaissance

Timeline in Weeks

1	2	3	4	5	6	7	8	9	10	11	12
Phase I Reconnaissance											
		Phase II Preparation									
				Phase III Ground War							
				Phase IV Air War							
								Campaign			

Phase I: Reconnaissance Dates (Start and End): _____

_____

_____

Phase II: Preparation   Dates (Start and End): _____

_____

_____

Phase III: Ground War   Dates (Start and End): _____

_____

_____

Phase IV: Air War Dates (Start and End): _____

_____

_____

Campaign   Dates (Start and End): _____

Estimating Your Raise

Preliminary Team Assessment

Partners

_____

_____

_____

_____

_____

_____

Champions

_____

_____

_____

_____

_____

_____

_____

_____

_____

_____

_____

Estimating Your Raise:

Number of Partners (from list above): _____ x $2,000 = _____

Number of Champions (from list above): _____ x $1,000 = _____

Total: Sum = _____

Assessing Your Cause

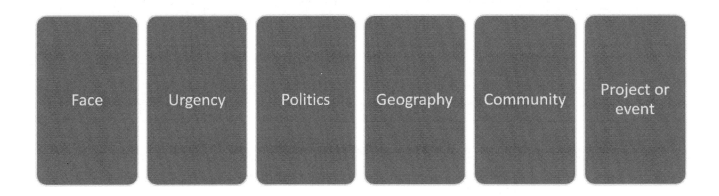

Score your cause on a 5-point scale:

Face	Urgency	Politics	Geography	Community	Project or event

My Notes   Date:_____

_____

_____

_____

_____

_____

_____

_____

_____

Face

Who is the face of your campaign? _____

What is the authentic connection between your face and your cause? _____

_____

Is (or was) the face of your campaign a living, breathing person or critter? _____

List the strengths and weaknesses of the face of your campaign. If the weaknesses outweigh the strengths, just find a new face!

Strengths	Weaknesses

Score:

With the help of honest feedback from others or at least being as objective as you can be, give your "face" a score on a scale from 1 to 5 where a 5 is the best. _____

Work online at bit.ly/cfsgworksheet

Urgency

What makes your campaign urgent? _____
_____
_____

Is your cause more like the Boston bombing or the American Cancer Society? Why?
_____
_____

List the strengths and weaknesses of the urgency of your campaign.

Strengths	Weaknesses

Score:

With the help of honest feedback from others or at least being as objective as you can be, give your "urgency" a score on a scale from 1 to 5 where a 5 is the best. _____

Work online at bit.ly/cfsgworksheet

Politics

What makes your campaign divisive? _____
_____
_____

What about your campaign is unifying? _____
_____
_____

List the strengths and weaknesses of the politics of your campaign.

Strengths	Weaknesses

Score:

With the help of honest feedback from others or at least being as objective as you can be, give your "politics" a score on a scale from 1 to 5 where a 5 is the best. _____

Work online at bit.ly/cfsgworksheet

Geography

What is the geography associated with your cause? _____
_____
_____

For whom is this cause local? _____
_____
_____

List the strengths and weaknesses of the geography of your campaign.

Strengths	Weaknesses

Score:

With the help of honest feedback from others or at least being as objective as you can be, give your "geography" a score on a scale from 1 to 5 where a 5 is the best. _____

Work online at bit.ly/cfsgworksheet

16

Community

What social communities are associated directly with your cause?_____

_____

_____

How will you communicate with these communities? _____

_____

_____

List the strengths and weaknesses of the communities related to your campaign.

Strengths	Weaknesses

Score:

With the help of honest feedback from others or at least being as objective as you can be, give your "community" a score on a scale from 1 to 5 where a 5 is the best. _____

Work online at bit.ly/cfsgworksheet

Project or Event

What specific project will you use the money you raise to complete?_____
_____
_____

What event associated with your campaign will you hold? _____
_____
_____

List the strengths and weaknesses of the project or event related to your campaign.

Strengths	Weaknesses

Score:

With the help of honest feedback from others or at least being as objective as you can be, give your "project or event" a score on a scale from 1 to 5 where a 5 is the best. _____

Work online at bit.ly/cfsgworksheet

Final Assessment

Enter the score you gave your campaign for each of the six points below.

Face	
Urgency	
Politics	
Geography	
Community	
Event	
Total	

According to Rockethub CEO Brian Meece, most campaigns raise about 25 percent of their funding from outside their network. A few, flip that ratio and get 75 percent from people outside the network, he says.

Based on my review of successful crowdfunding campaigns, you can reasonably expect to be part of the elite group of crowdfunders if you score 25 or more points on this self-assessment. Conversely, if you don't score at least 15 points, you may struggle to raise money beyond your network at all.

Work online at bit.ly/cfsgworksheet

My Notes

Date:_____

_____

_____

_____

_____

_____

_____

_____

_____

_____

_____

_____

_____

_____

_____

_____

_____

Adjusted Estimate of Your Campaign

Row 1: Initial Estimate	Campaign Estimate from page 11.	
Row 2: Your Campaign's Overall Appeal	Based on your total score on page 19, enter 1 if you scored 15 or below , .75 if you scored between 15 and 25, and .25 if you scored 25 or better.	
Row 3: Your Adjusted Campaign Estimate	Divide Row 1 by Row 2. For example, if you estimated $10,000 on page 11 and scored 20 on page 19, you would divide $10,000 by .75 to get $13,333.	

This exercise is intended to give you a sense of what you can realistically raise via crowdfunding. This is not a scientific formula and the only thing we can be certain of is that when you finish your campaign, you will have raised some other amount different than what was predicted, perhaps substantially. Your success will be a function of how much effort you make and how well you incorporate the lessons and strategies you learn today.

Work online at bit.ly/cfsgworksheet

So you want to raise $1 million?

- *Do you have a marketing budget of at least $100,000?*

- *Do you have an "A-list" celebrity signed on to actively promote your campaign?*

- *Do you have at 1 least million email addresses on your mailing list?*

- *Are many of your friends and followers passionate about what you are doing?*

- *Can you get national and international media attention?*

- *How lucky are you?*

Platform Considerations

My Notes   Date:_____

_____

_____

_____

_____

_____

_____

_____

My Notes

Date:_____

_____

_____

_____

_____

_____

_____

_____

_____

_____

_____

_____

_____

_____

_____

_____

_____

Timeline—Preparation

Timeline in Weeks

1	2	3	4	5	6	7	8	9	10	11	12
Phase I Reconnaissance											
		Phase II Preparation									
				Phase III Ground War							
				Phase IV Air War							
								Campaign			

My Notes   Date:_____

_____

_____

_____

_____

_____

_____

_____

Who Are Your Partners?

Name	Why Should They Be As Committed As I Am?	Date and Time Committed

Who Are Your Champions?

Name	Why Should They Be Passionate About My Cause?	Date and Time Committed

Work online at bit.ly/cfsgworksheet

Devin's Crowdfunding Training Resources

a.co/5b3Jm8a

bit.ly/2omRQmD

bit.ly/crowdfundingtraining

Check Devin's availability to personally train your group by sending an email to speaker@devinthorpe.com. If you paid to take his course, remind him and get a 10% discount off the standard $5,0000 fee.

Who Are Your Big Backers?

Name	Phone	Email

Work online at bit.ly/cfsgworksheet

Who Are Kindest Friends?

Name	Phone	Email
1		
2		
3		
4		
5		
6		
7		
8		
9		
10		
11		
12		
13		

Work online at bit.ly/cfsgworksheet

Who Are Kindest Friends?

Name	Phone	Email
16		
17		
18		
19		
20		
21		
22		
23		
24		
25		
26		
27		
28		
29		
30		

Work online at bit.ly/cfsgworksheet

Who are your 120 closest friends?

Name	Phone	Email
1		
2		
3		
4		
5		
6		
7		
8		
9		
10		
11		
12		
13		

Work online at bit.ly/cfsgworksheet

Who are your 120 closest friends?

Name	Phone	Email
16		
17		
18		
19		
20		
21		
22		
23		
24		
25		
26		
27		
28		
29		
30		

Work online at bit.ly/cfsgworksheet

Who are your 120 closest friends?

Name	Phone	Email
31		
32		
33		
34		
35		
36		
37		
38		
39		
40		
41		
42		
43		

Work online at bit.ly/cfsgworksheet

Who are your 120 closest friends?

Name	Phone	Email
46		
47		
48		
49		
50		
51		
52		
53		
54		
55		
56		
57		
58		
59		
60		

Work online at bit.ly/cfsgworksheet

Who are your 120 closest friends?

Name	Phone	Email
61		
62		
63		
64		
65		
66		
67		
68		
69		
70		
71		
72		
73		

Work online at bit.ly/cfsgworksheet

Who are your 120 closest friends?

Name	Phone	Email
76		
77		
78		
79		
80		
81		
82		
83		
84		
85		
86		
87		
88		
89		
90		

Work online at bit.ly/cfsgworksheet

Who are your 120 closest friends?

Name	Phone	Email
91		
92		
93		
94		
95		
96		
97		
98		
99		
100		
101		
102		
103		

Work online at bit.ly/cfsgworksheet

Who are your 120 closest friends?

Name	Phone	Email
106		
107		
108		
109		
110		
111		
112		
113		
114		
115		
116		
117		
118		
119		
120		

Work online at bit.ly/cfsgworksheet

My Rewards for My Backers

Reward Description	Price: What does the backer pay you?	Cost:: What does it cost you to produce, receive, package and deliver the reward?	Gross Profit: Price - Cost = Gross Profit

Press Release Template

Title (Up to 100 Characters)	
Subtitle (Up to 25 Words)	
Introductory Paragraph	
Supporting Paragraph	
Quote #1	
Quote #2	
About The Company with Link to Website	
###	
Contact Information (Name, Title, email, phone, address)	

Media Contacts and Bloggers

Name	Phone	Email	Publication/Show
1			
2			
3			
4			
5			
6			
7			
8			
9			
10			
11			
12			
13			

Crowdfunding Video

youtu.be/l4irb2K1p8E

PROJECT
RENEWAL

Renewing lives. Reclaiming hope.

youtu.be/liZBAz4gEiU

_____

_____

_____

_____

_____

_____

_____

_____

_____

_____

_____

_____

_____

_____

_____

_____

_____

_____

_____

_____

_____

_____

_____

_____

_____

_____

_____

_____

_____

_____

_____

_____

_____

_____

_____

_____

_____

_____

_____

_____

_____

_____

_____

_____

_____

_____

_____

_____

_____

Timeline—Ground War

Timeline in Weeks

1	2	3	4	5	6	7	8	9	10	11	12
Phase I Reconnaissance											
		Phase II Preparation									
				Phase III Ground War							
				Phase IV Air War							
								Campaign			

My Notes   Date:_____

_____

_____

_____

_____

_____

_____

Big Backers

Name	When	Where

Big Backer Math

5 of 10 take a meeting

3 of 5 Give

3 * 500 = $1,500

(Your success rates will vary.)

Work the Phones

Call the people on your list of kindest friends (pages 30 and 31).

My Notes   Date:_____

_____

_____

_____

_____

_____

Draft an Email to Your Mother

_____

_____

_____

_____

_____

_____

_____

_____

_____

_____

_____

_____

_____

_____

Mail Merge

Gmail and Google Drive

1. Draft an email in Gmail

2. Make a email list in Google Drive Sheets

3. Add sentence-length custom greetings and personalization

4. Add In: Yet Another Mail Merge

5. Enter merge fields in draft email with <<Column Head>> syntax

6. Add In: Start Mail Merge (follow prompts to send)

Microsoft Outlook with Word and Excel

1. Make a email list in Excel

2. Add sentence-length custom greetings and personalization (save)

3. Start Word and open Mailing tab

4. Click Start Mail Merge

5. Select your Excel list of names and emails

6. In Word, enter merge fields in draft email using "Insert Merge Field" button

7. Complete the email

8. Click Preview Results (check to see that all merge fields and personalization is working)

9. Click Finish & Merge (follow prompts to send)

Mail merge should make your task of sending 120 personal emails easier. If this looks too intimidating, just edit each email to all of your friends to personalize it before sending and don't worry about the mail merge.

Whatever you do, don't bcc all 120 of your friends on an email to your mother!

Pledge Log

	Name	Email	Pledge
1			
2			
3			
4			
5			
6			
7			
8			
9			
10			
11			
12			
13			
14			
15			

Work online at bit.ly/cfsgworksheet

Pledge Log

Name	Email	Pledge
16		
17		
18		
19		
20		
21		
22		
23		
24		
25		
26		
27		
28		

Work online at bit.ly/cfsgworksheet

Timeline—Air War & Campaign

Timeline in Weeks

1	2	3	4	5	6	7	8	9	10	11	12
Phase I Reconnaissance											
		Phase II Preparation									
				Phase III Ground War							
				Phase IV Air War							
								Campaign			

My Notes

Date:_____

_____

_____

_____

_____

_____

_____

_____

Draft Email to the Media

Use their name:	
Praise their work genuinely ad specifically:	
Explain the connection between their topic and yours:	
Explain why your subject is so interesting:	
Offer to be available for an interview or to provide additional information:	
Include your contact information:	
Provide your Press Release in the text of the email:	
Provide a link to photos and video and offer to provide them by email:	

Plan a Kick-off Party

Time and Date	
Location: (Cheap or free)	
How will people far away participate?	
How can people at the party donate?	
Will you charge admission? Charge for drinks? For food?	
What is your hashtag?	
What is the big photo op?	
What rewards will you offer to people for using social media?	
How will you invite people to sign up as Boosters (fundraisers)?	
What incentives will you announce and offer to Boosters and Champions?	
What will you do to ensure everyone has fun?	
Who will perform?	
How else will you ensure that everyone remembers this is a party?	

Second Email to the Media

Use their name:	
Praise their work genuinely and specifically; refer to a more recent piece:	
Breifly explain the connection between their topic and yours:	
Explain your tremendous progress since your last email.	
Offer to be available for an interview or to provide additional information:	
Include your contact information:	
Provide a new Press Release in the text of the email:	
Provide a link to photos and video and offer to provide them by email:	

The Social Media Campaign

My Notes   Date:_____

_____

_____

_____

_____

_____

_____

_____

_____

Daily Social Media Planner

Draft a short post for each day

1

2

3

4

5

6

7

8

9

10

11

12

13

Work online at bit.ly/cfsgworksheet

Daily Social Media Planner

Draft a short post for each day

1

2

3

4

5

6

7

8

9

10

11

12

13

14

15

Work online at bit.ly/cfsgworksheet

Advertising on Facebook

Advertising Basics

- Pick posts on your Facebook page that got the most attention

- "Boost" them

- Start with tiny amounts of money

- See which boosted post performs best

- Invest more in the best ad

- Make a slight variation and test again

- After testing, only continue if advertising generates much more money than you're spending

Choosing the Right Audience

- Reach your friends by advertising to people who like your page and their friends

- Reach people who care about your cause by advertising to people who have liked giant organizations that support your cause

- Download your Linkedin connections and upload them to Facebook as a custom audience

- Download your organization's email list and upload that as a custom audience

- Create a look alike audience (a list of millions of people with similar interests to your email subscribers)

Make a Coordinated Push

My Notes   Date:_____

_____

_____

_____

_____

_____

_____

_____

The Story of Vivienne Harr

Watch the story of Vivienne Harr's impact and crowd-funding success: youtu.be/eLdoR8ldTrc.

Is Investment Crowdfunding Right for You?

My Notes   Date: _____

_____

_____

_____

_____

_____

_____

_____

_____

_____

_____

_____

_____

_____

_____

_____

My Notes

Date:_____

_____

_____

_____

_____

_____

_____

_____

_____

_____

_____

_____

_____

_____

_____

_____

_____

The Story of Elio Motors

Watch the story of Elio Motors: https://youtu.be/GYzoWbsBq8s.

Experts Explain New Crowdfunding Rules

By Devin Thorpe

Late last month, the SEC kept its word from late 2014 when it said it would issue final rules for Regulation Crowdfunding under the JOBS Act by October 2015.

Todd Crosland, CEO and Founder of Seed Equity Ventures, a broker dealer already operating and doing crowdfunding type equity raises under the SEC's Regulation D 506(c) rules for general solicitations, says, " I believe the SEC passing Title III will be a watershed event for both startups and investors. Startups and the general investing public will be forever changed."

Crosland explains the import of the new rules, "The purpose is to allow non accredited investors the ability to invest in startups, which was once only reserved for the elite few."

The rules are final, but they aren't effective, yet. As Crosland notes, "Once the rules go live on May 16, 2016 and Seed Equity's platform is approved by the SEC and Finra, non-accredited investors will be able to invest through the Seed Equity platform."

EnergyFunders will operate as a "platform" rather than as a broker-dealer under the new Regulation Crowdfunding rules, giving ordinary investors an opportunity to invest in oil and gas investments for the first time.

EnergyFunders founder Philip Racusin says, "We hope to educate investors and provide them transparent access to an elite asset class which was previously inaccessible for many. We also hope to attract more small operators to use our platform, which will provide them project funding traditionally denied to them by banks."

Many in the small business and startup arenas have hoped that there would be many crowdfunding platforms like EnergyFunders. Draft rules issued by the SEC in 2013 were disappointing to many and some players left the space or pivoted to other opportunities. It may be too soon to tell whether the new rules will yet create the intended jobs.

One of the biggest stumbling blocks in the draft rules, an audit requirement for companies wishing to raise more than $500,000, was amended in the final regulations such that an audit is required only for a second raise under the rules. A formal review is still required for all raises of $100,000 or more.

On Thursday, November 19, 2015 at 3:00 Eastern, Racusin and Crossland will join me for a live discussion about the new rules. We will be joined by Jason Best, one of the authors of the JOBS Act, attorney Douglas Ellenoff, and public relations pro Joy Schoffler. Tune in here (*youtu.be/sEy4ula1apw*) then to watch the interview live. Post questions in the comments below or tweet questions before the interview to @devindthorpe.

More about Leverage PR:

> Twitter: @leverage_pr

> Leverage PR is an Austin-based full-service public relations firm that delivers strategic planning, media relations and communications strategies to companies within the financial, legal, real estate and technology industries.

Schoffler's bio:

> Twitter: @joyschoffler

> Joy Schoffler, principal of Leverage PR, is a nationally recognized author and speaker in

the field of innovative financial services marketing and communication. Prior to launching Leverage PR, Joy served as director of acquisitions for the Inc. award-winning private equity firm. Joy has written for a number of publications including: Entrepreneur.com, Social Media Monthly and MarketingProfs, among other outlets. She is a contributing author for the Wiley-published Bloomberg Media book "Crowdfunding: The Ultimate Guide to Raising Capital on the Internet." Her expertise in helping issuers and investment firms market themselves to the accredited investment community has additionally led to Joy being featured in a number of outlets including: CNBC, Forbes, Inc., Reuters, Yahoo! Small Business and dozens of other niche sites.

More about Energy Funders:

Twitter: @EnergyFunders

EnergyFunders is an online marketplace that connects qualified investors to nationwide, small cap oil and gas projects managed by proven operators. Developed by experienced securities attorneys and trusted specialists in the oil and gas industry, EnergyFunders is the first platform to offer global and national participation in the $263 billion "small oil" market through equity crowdfunding, allowing investors to buy directly into wells themselves for investment minimums as low as $5,000. Managing assets of more than one hundred wells, the company has raised millions for projects, bringing unprecedented access, transparency and efficiency to one of the most elite and lucrative asset classes.

Racusin's bio:

Twitter: @philipracusin

Philip Racusin is the CEO and co-founder of EnergyFunders, an online marketplace that connects qualified investors to nationwide, small cap oil and gas projects managed by proven operators. A seasoned litigation attorney, Philip currently serves as a senior associate of Pagel, Davis & Hill, P.C., where he has successfully represented clients, ranging from individuals to large companies, in a variety of legal disputes for nearly a decade. He also launched several startup ventures prior to EnergyFunders, including a legal technology company that totaled over 50,000% ROI in one year. Both a savvy entrepreneur and accomplished litigator, Philip fuses legal expertise with astute business knowhow to navigate the oil and gas industry's regulatory waters and carefully pre-vet each project offered through the site.

More about Seed Equity Ventures:

Twitter: @getseedequity

Seed Equity Ventures is a registered broker dealer with the U.S. Securities and Exchange Commission and is a member of both FINRA and SIPC. Seed Equity Ventures provides investment banking services to startups and growth companies from around the world.

Crosland's bio:

Twitter: @toddcrosland

A seasoned entrepreneur, Mr. Crosland has demonstrated the ability to build successful teams and companies. Mr. Crosland was the Founder, Chairman and CEO of Interbank FX, LLC ("IBFX"), from 2001 until he sold the firm in 2011. IBFX was a Futures Commission Merchant and Retail Foreign Exchange Dealer registered with the U.S. Commodities Futures Trading Commission. IBFX was also authorized and regulated by the Australian Securities and Investments Commission. IBFX was a worldwide leader in retail

Forex trading services. IBFX offered individual traders, fund managers and institutional customer's proprietary technology and tools to trade Forex online. IBFX saw Global customers grow to over 40,000, in more than 140 countries. Annual trading volume reached $750 billion. IBFX had 120 employees and offices in Beijing, China; Seoul, South Korea; Sydney, Australia; Salt Lake City, Utah and London, England. Mr. Crosland holds a B.A. in Business (Business Finance) from the University of Utah. He also currently holds the following Securities Licenses: Series 7, 24, and 63 and previously held series 3 and 30 Licenses.

More about Ellenoff Grossman & Schole LLP:

Ellenoff Grossman & Schole LLP is a New York City-based law firm comprised of over 65 professionals, offering its clients legal services in a broad range of business related matters. Founded in 1992, the Firm specializes in many areas of commercial law: Corporate, Securities, Private Investment Funds, Broker-Dealer Regulation, Real Estate, Labor and Employment, Intellectual Property, Litigation, Arbitration, Tax and Estate Planning.

Ellenoff's bio:

Douglas Ellenoff serves as the co-founder of iDisclose, an adaptive web-based application that enables entrepreneurs to prepare customized institutional grade private placement documents for a fraction of the time and cost. A highly esteemed corporate and securities attorney for more than two decades, Doug also serves as founding partner of Ellenoff, Grossman & Schole, a finance law firm known as a leader in crowdfunding, where he has facilitated several billion dollars in transactions for dozens of broker-dealers, investor groups and small businesses. As one of the world's most prominent figures in crowdfunding, Doug was a key player in the implementation of JOBS Act regulations. A sought after speaker and media source on innovative capital formation, Doug is passionate about placing high quality legal disclosure within any businesses' reach.

More about Crowdfund Capital Advisors:

Crowdfund Capital Advisors (CCA) delivers strategic insights to government agencies, financial institutions, and professional investors seeking to both create and implement innovative strategies to utilize crowdfund investing (CFI) technologies to drive innovation, job creation and entrepreneurship. They also study and invest in the emerging ecosystem of crowdfunding and the new solutions being created that will impact the broader private capital markets. The social web has changed the way individuals businesses, and governments organize and communicate and transact business. We are passionate about creating innovation, entrepreneurship and jobs through the use of crowdfunding. CCA delivers strategic services and implementation programs that create, proprietary deal flow for professional investors, better access to capital for businesses, and policy and regulatory innovation for governments.

Best's bio:

As co-founder and principal of Crowdfund Capital Advisors (CCA), Jason Best co-authored the crowdfund investing framework used in the JOBS Act to legalize equity and debt based crowdfunding in the USA. He has provided congressional testimony on crowdfunding and was honored to attend the White House ceremony when President Obama signed the JOBS Act into law on April 5, 2012. Jason co-founded the crowdfunding industry trade group that works with the Securities and Exchange Commission and FINRA as they create the rules for crowdfund investing. Jason also works with angel groups, PE/VC firms as well as governments and NGOs, including The World Bank, to understand the crowdfunding ecosystem and create successful crowdfund investing strategies. He was instrumental in the successful effort to have CCA selected by the US State Department's Global Entrepreneurship Program as a Key Partner.

This article original appeared on Forbes.com at http://bit.ly/2n2deAM.

Watch the live interview: youtu.be/sEy4ula1apw.

Investment Crowdfunding: What Works And What Needs Fixing

By Devin Thorpe

On May 16, 2016, Regulation Crowdfunding became effective. Arguably representing the biggest change to securities laws in 80 years, Title III of the JOBS Act passed in 2012 made investment crowdfunding legal subject to the issuance of regulations. Now, almost five years after the law passed, we have enough history with the rules to begin understanding what's working and what's not.

To work through the issues, I reached out to leading crowdfunding practitioners and experts for their reactions to the first nine months of practice in the space.

Bernard Loyd, a social entrepreneur and President of Urban Juncture, Inc., was among those who have had good experiences with the new rules. "Our experience has been that it provides efficient access to a broad pool of potential investors, many previously unknown to us. The online platform provides significantly better access to potential investors who share our passion for investing in economically-challenged, under-resourced urban enterprises with whom we otherwise would not have been able to connect."

There is consensus that while Regulation Crowdfunding is working for some issuers, changes in the law or regulation would allow it to work for more entrepreneurs. Joy Schoffler is the Principal of Leverage PR, which represents clients in the crowdfunding space. Her reaction was typical, "I see it working for many companies already."

The biggest challenge with the rules is the $1 million cap on crowdfunding offering. David Weild, IV, Chairman and CEO of Weild & Co., said, "The gross proceeds cap of $1 million is overly limiting. It should be eliminated altogether. Remember, there is a dollar-exposure-limitation ($5,000) per non-accredited investor so there is no need to limit the aggregate raise. Why do we care if there are 200 investors at $5,000 each or 20,000 investors at $5,000 each when the individual investor has the same risk limit? It is an arbitrary and poorly thought-through limitation."

Kendall Almerico, a JOBS Act and crowdfunding attorney, largely agrees. "Congress set the $1 million limit far too low. It should be raised to at least $5 million."

Alon Goren, Co-Founder, Crowd invest Summit, would go one step further, eliminating the restrictions on individual investors. "I think that anyone should be able to invest in what they want. I think that the limits are un-American, both on the size of the raise and on the investor."

Congress is working on fixes, notes Philip Racusin, CEO of EnergyFunders. "The Fix Crowdfunding Act is a start in that it would allow for the use of special purpose vehicles to aggregate together investors (for the benefit of the investors and the business owner), and raises the maximum fundraise to $5,000,000."

Special purpose vehicles or SPVs are used to manage large numbers of small investors, simplifying the capitalization table and ownership structure from the perspective of the issuer. SPVs are specifically prohibited by the current rules. Sara Hanks, CEO of CrowdCheck, and Douglas Ellenoff, Partner at Ellenoff Grossman & Schole LLP, a crowdfunding lawyer, agree that allowing SPVs is a necessary fix.

Another problem with the rules that experts say needs to be fixed is the prohibition on testing the waters. Title IV of the JOBS Act authorized the SEC to issue new rules for Regulation A offerings, raising the limits and specifically allowing issuers to expose a potential offering to the market publicly before launching the offering formally, even allowing the issuer to collect formal, non-binding expressions of interest in advance.

Hanks, Vincent Bradley, former CEO of FlashFunders, and Dan Baird, CEO of Crack the Crowd, among others, agree that adding testing the waters to Regulation Crowdfunding is essential.

Almerico explains why, saying, "No pre-launch marketing is allowed, which prevents a company from effectively soliciting investors until the offering is live. With a rewards-based campaign on Indiegogo or Kickstarter, successful companies spend months conditioning the market, generating leads and building up social capital before their launch. You cannot do that with Reg CF, and it means a company is behind the eight ball when they start their offering, because their marketing has not even begun yet." He notes that the SEC has unilateral authority to change this rule.

Several practitioners, including, Weild, note that the limitations on marketing a crowdfunding campaign even after it launches are unnecessarily strict. "Don't you find it fascinating," he says, "that anyone can sell anything (except securities) on Kickstarter without limitation and buyers are given zero upside for their purchase money and the companies are only subject to criminal fraud? Regulation Crowdfunding gives the buyer upside. Why should securities be treated so differently from commerce, especially for smaller companies? There is no systemic risk concern for Government."

Jenny Kassan, an attorney who consults with social entrepreneurs and women-led businesses on capital strategies including crowdfunding, noted, the marketing "restrictions are nonsensical," adding, "this could be done without legislation."

The JOBS Act requires crowdfunding issuers to file an annual report with the SEC. Kassan believes this requirement should be lifted, noting, "I think this would require legislation."

While the rules do not define any of the costs of a crowdfunding offering, the rules do impose costs. Racusin highlighted the need to reduce the regulatory burden to reduce the costs of offerings, especially those over $500,000.

Among the other lessons learned, Weild noted, "The $1 million cap is not large enough to entice broker dealers and investment bankers to become involved so they don't and the companies really could use the advice/involvement of experienced professionals."

As the crowdfunding rules were being drafted, there was a lot of discussion about fraud and the corollary need to protect crowdfunding investors from it. Ellenoff noted, "That all of the expressed concern over fraud has not borne out as a legitimate reason for frustrating the legislation."

Scott Picken, founder and CEO of Wealth Migrate, similarly noted, "There is significant demand and while the regulation is important to ensure that the consumer is protected, social proofing also goes a long way to protecting the consumer." He added, "Most importantly investing is common sense and everyone has common sense."

Mika Onishi and Emi Onishi, founders of UpToGood, a crowdfunding site for filmmakers, noted, "It appears that valuations for companies raising through equity crowdfunding is in line with VC valued companies which is encouraging." They also noted, the "size of social network seems to matter predictably on the success of the fundraising campaign."

Josef Holm, founder Krowdster, noted, "Crowd investors need to be marketed to just like any Kickstarter or Indiegogo backer. This means it takes time, a marketing budget and hands-on involvement by the founders to build an excited crowd that will actually invest."

Not everyone agrees that the current rules are workable. Sally Outlaw, Founder of Peerbackers, said, "Securities do not sell themselves and there are so many hurdles that it's tough to even get entrepreneurs excited about using this option [Regulation Crowdfunding]."

Goren provided some insight for determining when it works and when it doesn't. "If your company doesn't sell a product or service that can be sold to consumers on the internet it will probably fail. If your company does not fit that criteria and you want to use crowdfunding just because it is a good investment opportunity and you think crowdfunding sounds easy, you are probably wasting time and resources."

This article originally appeared on Forbes at http://bit.ly/2nP9SzL.

My Notes

Date:_____

My Notes

Date:_____

_____

_____

_____

_____

_____

_____

_____

_____

_____

_____

_____

_____

_____

_____

_____

_____

_____

My Notes

Date:_____

_____

_____

_____

_____

_____

_____

_____

_____

_____

_____

_____

_____

_____

_____

_____

My Notes

Date:_____

_____

_____

_____

_____

_____

_____

_____

_____

_____

_____

_____

_____

_____

_____

_____

_____

My Notes

Date:_____

_____

_____

_____

_____

_____

_____

_____

_____

_____

_____

_____

_____

_____

_____

_____

My Notes

Date:_____

_____

_____

_____

_____

_____

_____

_____

_____

_____

_____

_____

_____

_____

_____

_____

_____

My Notes

Date:_____

My Notes

Date:_____

My Notes

Date:_____

My Notes

Date:_____

_____

_____

_____

_____

_____

_____

_____

_____

_____

_____

_____

_____

_____

_____

_____

_____

My Notes

Date:_____

_____

_____

_____

_____

_____

_____

_____

_____

_____

_____

_____

_____

_____

_____

_____

_____

_____

My Notes

Date:_____

_____

_____

_____

_____

_____

_____

_____

_____

_____

_____

_____

_____

_____

_____

_____

_____

_____

My Notes

Date:_____

_____

_____

_____

_____

_____

_____

_____

_____

_____

_____

_____

_____

_____

_____

_____

My Notes

Date:_____

_____

_____

_____

_____

_____

_____

_____

_____

_____

_____

_____

_____

_____

_____

_____

_____

My Notes

Date:_____

My Notes

Date:_____

_____

_____

_____

_____

_____

_____

_____

_____

_____

_____

_____

_____

_____

_____

_____

_____

My Notes

Date:_____

_____

_____

_____

_____

_____

_____

_____

_____

_____

_____

_____

_____

_____

_____

_____

_____

My Notes

Date:_____

My Notes

Date:_____

_____

_____

_____

_____

_____

_____

_____

_____

_____

_____

_____

_____

_____

_____

_____

_____

My Notes

Date:_____

_____

_____

_____

_____

_____

_____

_____

_____

_____

_____

_____

_____

_____

_____

_____

_____

My Notes

Date:_____

_____

_____

_____

_____

_____

_____

_____

_____

_____

_____

_____

_____

_____

_____

_____

My Notes

Date:_____

_____

_____

_____

_____

_____

_____

_____

_____

_____

_____

_____

_____

_____

_____

_____

_____

My Notes

Date:_____

_____

_____

_____

_____

_____

_____

_____

_____

_____

_____

_____

_____

_____

_____

_____

_____

My Notes

Date:_____

_____

_____

_____

_____

_____

_____

_____

_____

_____

_____

_____

_____

_____

_____

_____

My Notes

Date:_____

My Notes

Date:_____

My Notes

Date:_____

My Notes

Date:_____

My Notes

Date:_____

_____

_____

_____

_____

_____

_____

_____

_____

_____

_____

_____

_____

_____

_____

_____

My Notes

Date:_____

_____

_____

_____

_____

_____

_____

_____

_____

_____

_____

_____

_____

_____

_____

My Notes

Date:_____

_____

_____

_____

_____

_____

_____

_____

_____

_____

_____

_____

_____

_____

_____

_____

_____

_____

My Notes

Date:_____

_____

_____

_____

_____

_____

_____

_____

_____

_____

_____

_____

_____

_____

_____

_____

_____

My Notes

Date:_____

_____

_____

_____

_____

_____

_____

_____

_____

_____

_____

_____

_____

_____

_____

_____

_____

My Notes

Date:_____

_____

_____

_____

_____

_____

_____

_____

_____

_____

_____

_____

_____

_____

_____

_____

_____

_____

Corporate Social Responsibility Speaker

To check Devin's availability, call 801-930-0588 or send an email to speaker@devinthorpe.com.

Devin's keynote presentation "Adding Profit by Adding Purpose," based on his book by the same name, is both inspirational and informative.

- You will see that you can make a profit by adding purpose to your organization

- You will learn how to authentically choose a cause to engage your customers and employees

- You will discover several ways you can share the costs of purpose programs with your customers

As a new-media journalist and founder of the Your Mark on the World Center, Devin has established himself as a champion of social good. As a Forbes contributor, with 400 bylines and over one million unique visitors, he has become a recognized name in the social impact arena. His YouTube show, featuring over 800 celebrities, CEOs, billionaires, entrepreneurs and others who are out to change the world, gives him a recognizable face as well.

Previously, Devin served as the CFO of the third largest company on the 2009 Inc. 500 list. He also founded and led an NASD-registered investment bank. After completing a degree in finance at the University of Utah, he earned an MBA from Cornell University.

Having lived on three continents and visited over 30 countries on six continents and with guests from around the world on his show, Devin brings a global perspective to audiences around the world–from the UN to Nepal–empowering them to do more good and make their mark on the world. These lessons also enable them to change their personal lives and to drive positive change within their organizations. His books provide roadmaps to audiences on how to use money for good. His books have been over 1 million times!

Today, Devin channels the idealism of his youth, volunteering whenever and wherever he can, with the loving support of his wife, Gail. Their son, Dayton, is a PhD candidate in Physics at UC Berkeley.

Watch Devin's speech at the United Nations here: youtu.be/YuZM-fGMIhQ.

68064252R00061

Made in the USA
Lexington, KY
30 September 2017